W9-BKE-190

GAIL BORDEN
Public Library District
270 N. Grove Avenue
Elgin, Illinois 60120
(847) 742-2411

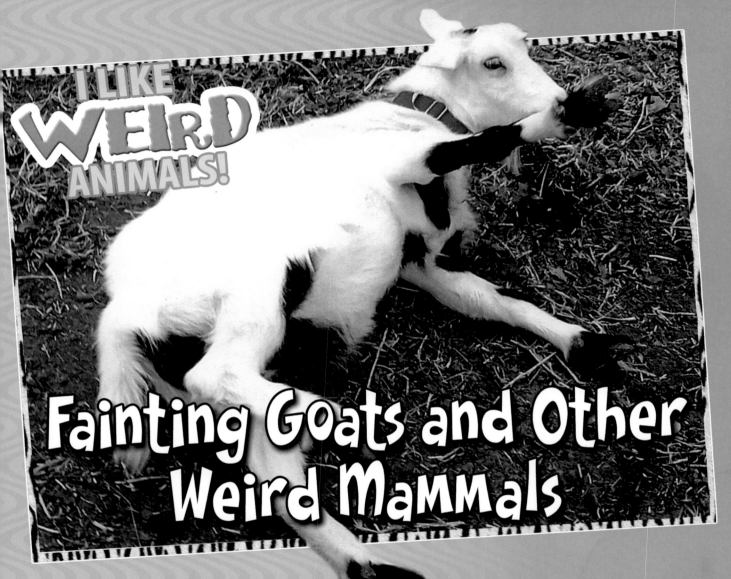

I LIKE WEIRD ANIMALS!

Fainting Goats and Other Weird Mammals

Carmen Bredeson

ies Science Consultant:
nnis L. Claussen, PhD
fessor of Zoology
ami University
ford, OH

Series Literacy Consultant:
Allan A. De Fina, PhD
Dean, College of Education/Professor of Literacy Education
New Jersey City University
Past President of the New Jersey Reading Association

CONTENTS

WORDS TO KNOW

enemy (EH nuh mee)—An animal that tries to hurt or kill another animal.

fainting (FAYN ting)—Feeling weak and passing out.

mammals (MA muls)—Living things that drink milk from their mothers when they are babies.

muscles (MUH suls)—Body parts that make animals move.

tentacles (TEN tuh kuls)—Long feelers on the head or mouth of an animal.

WEIRD MAMMALS

Mammals live all over the world.

People are mammals.

So are dogs, elephants, and whales.

Some mammals look strange.

Others do strange things.

Which mammal is your favorite?

The vampire bat is the only bat that drinks BLOOD!

FAINTING GOAT

When these goats get excited, they fall over onto the ground.

Their **muscles** freeze and DOWN they go.

After a few minutes, their muscles relax.

Then the goats can get up and run around again.

Duck-Billed Platypus

A platypus [PLA tih pus] looks and acts like many different animals.

It has a beak and webbed feet like a duck.

It has a tail like a beaver's.

Platypus babies hatch from eggs, like birds!

STAR-NOSED MOLE

This mole is nearly blind.

It digs in the dirt with its long claws.

Then the 22 **tentacles** on its nose feel around in the dirt.

The tentacles find worms and insects for the mole to eat.

Pygmy Marmoset

Pygmy marmosets (PIG mee MAR muh sets) are tiny monkeys.

The babies are as big as a person's THUMB.

Marmosets like to eat sap from trees.

First they chew a hole in the bark.

Then they lap up the sweet juice.

GIANT ANTEATER

This mammal is an ant-eating machine.

Its tongue slurps up about 30,000 ants every day.

The sticky tongue is as long as a person's ARM!

The anteater does not have teeth.

It swallows the ants whole.

THREE-TOED SLOTH

The sloth lives UPSIDE DOWN, hanging from a tree branch.

It eats, sleeps, and even has babies upside down.

Sloths move very, very slowly.

They spend most of their time sleeping. *Snore.*

THREE-BANDED ARMADILLO

WATCH OUT! Here comes an **enemy**.

A three-banded armadillo (ar muh DIH loh) tucks its head, legs, and tail into its shell.

The strong shell snaps shut.

The armadillo rolls into a ball.

Now the armadillo is safe.

TASMANIAN DEVIL

These animals open their mouths WIDE!

They have very strong teeth.

They can even eat bones!

Tasmanian (taz MAY nee in) devils scream and growl while they eat.

This is to scare other animals away from their food.

LEARN MORE

Books

Kalman, Bobbie. *Animals Called Mammals*. New York: Crabtree Publishing Company, 2005.

Phillips, Dee. *Mammals*. Minnetonka, Minn.: Two-Can Publishing, 2006.

Schulte, Mary. *Monkeys and Other Mammals*. New York: Children's Press, 2005.

LEARN MORE

Web Sites

Enchanted Learning
<http://www.enchantedlearning.com/subjects/mammals/>

National Geographic
<http://animals.nationalgeographic.com>
  Click on "mammals."

INDEX

For my weird siblings: Ralph, Jack, and Renee

Enslow Elementary, an imprint of Enslow Publishers, Inc.
Enslow Elementary® is a registered trademark of Enslow Publishers, Inc.

Copyright © 2010 by Carmen Bredeson

All rights reserved.

No part of this book may be reproduced by any means without the written permission of the publisher.

Library of Congress Cataloging-in-Publication Data

Bredeson, Carmen.
   Fainting goats and other weird mammals / Carmen Bredeson.
      p. cm. — (I like weird animals!)
   Summary: "Provides young readers with facts about several strange mammals"—Provided by publisher.
   ISBN-13: 978-0-7660-3122-7
   ISBN-10: 0-7660-3122-5
   1. Mammals—Miscellanea—Juvenile literature. I. Title.
   QL739.2.B74 2010
   599—dc22   20080214

Printed in the United States of America

10 9 8 7 6 5 4 3 2 1

To Our Readers: We have done our best to make sure all Internet Addresses in this book were active and appropriate when we went to press. However, the author and the publisher have no control over and assume no liability for the material available on those Internet sites or on other Web sites they may link to. Any comments or suggestions can be sent by e-mail to comments@enslow.com or to the address on the back cover.

♺ Enslow Publishers, Inc., is committed to printing our books on recycled paper. The paper in every book contains 10% to 30% post-consumer waste (PCW). The cover board on the outside of each book contains 100% PCW. Our goal is to do our part to help young people and the environment too!

Every effort has been made to locate all copyright holders of material used in this book. If any errors or omissions have occurred, corrections will be made in future editions of this book.

Photo Credits: Courtesy Becky Smith, Back 40 Game Farm, p. 1; Davewattsphoto.com, p. 21; Jacob Maentz, p. 6; Minden Pictures: Michael & Patricia Fogden, pp. 5, 17; Tui De Roy, p. 14; ZSSD, pp. 2, 15; Naturepl.com: Pete Oxford, p. 13; OceanwideImages.com: Gary Bell, p. 9; Photo Researchers, Inc.: Francois Gohier, p. 18; Rod Planck, p. 10.

Cover Photo: Courtesy Becky Smith, Back 40 Game Farm

Series Science Consultant:
Dennis L. Claussen, PhD
Professor of Zoology
Department of Zoology
Miami University
Oxford, OH

Series Literacy Consultant:
Allan A. De Fina, PhD
Dean, College of Education/ Professor of Literacy Education
New Jersey City University
Jersey City, NJ
Past President of the New Jersey Reading Association

Note to Parents and Teachers: The *I Like Weird Animals!* series supports the National Science Education Standards for K–4 science. The Words to Know section introduces subject-specific vocabulary words, including pronunciation and definitions. Early readers may need help with these new words.

Enslow Elementary
an imprint of
Enslow Publishers, Inc.
E | 40 Industrial Road
Box 398
Berkeley Heights, NJ 07922
USA
http://www.enslow.com